ALL ABOUT INSTAGRAM THREADS

WWW.DOKETS.SHOP

TABLE OF CONTENTS

- OVERVIEW   - PAGE 3

- THREADS TO MILLIONS: STRATEGY FOR
  INSTAGRAM THREADS

(A) CREATE VALUE-DRIVEN CONTENT- PAGE 5

(B) ENGAGE WITH INTERACTIVE ELEMENTS -PAGE 12

(C) CONSISTENT POSTING SCHEDULE - PAGE 19

(D) LEVERAGE VISUALS - PAGE 27

(E) OPTIMIZE FOR VIRALITY - PAGE 41

(F) ANALYZE AND REFINE - PAGE 54

- EXAMPLE - PAGE 68

- WHY IT WORKS - PAGE 69

OVERVIEW

IN THE WORLD OF INSTAGRAM THREADS, "THREADS TO MILLIONS" MEANS MAKING STUFF THAT USES THE COOL FORMAT OF THE PLATFORM.

IT'S ALL ABOUT GETTING ATTENTION, MAKING FOLKS INTERESTED, AND TURNING THEM INTO A BIG BUNCH OF FOLLOWERS. THIS CAN MAKE YOUR AUDIENCE AND MONEY GROW BIG TIME.

GIST OF INSTAGRAM THREADS

SO, INSTAGRAM THREADS IS THIS PLACE WHERE YOU CAN POST SHORT CHAT-LIKE THINGS, LIKE YOU DO ON TWITTER.

YOU GET TO DROP A BUNCH OF MESSAGES, OR "THREADS," THAT TELL A STORY OR SPILL THE BEANS ON SOMETHING CHUNKY. IT'S BUILT TO MAKE PEOPLE WANNA HIT THE LIKE, DROP COMMENTS AND SHARE THE LOVE.

"THREADS TO MILLIONS" STRATEGY FOR INSTAGRAM THREADS

CREATE VALUE-DRIVEN CONTENT

CREATING VALUE-BASED CONTENT FOR INSTAGRAM THREADS MEANS MAKING POSTS THAT RESONATE WITH YOUR TARGET AUDIENCE, ENGAGING THEM WITH WHAT YOU HAVE TO SAY.

THIS IS HOW YOU DO IT:

1. KNOW YOUR AUDIENCE

• KNOW YOUR NICHE:

KNOW WHAT YOUR TARGET AUDIENCE IS STRUGGLING WITH, WHAT THEY ARE INTERESTED IN, AND WHAT THEY ARE CURRENTLY LOOKING TO SOLVE OR BE EDUCATED ABOUT. WITH A NICHE OF HERBS AND AYURVEDA, WHAT HEALTH OR WELLNESS TOPICS ARE THEY AFTER?

• TREND RESEARCH:

IDENTIFY THE TRENDING TOPICS OR FREQUENTLY ASKED QUESTIONS IN YOUR NICHE AND CREATE CONTENT THAT IS IN LINE WITH THE CURRENT INTERESTS.

2. RELATED TOPIC CHOICE

- YOU MUST CONCENTRATE MORE ON RELATED TOPICS THAT BENEFIT YOUR READERS' LIVES, SUCH AS WELLNESS TIPS, SOME HERBS THAT ARE BENEFICIAL, OR AYURVEDIC PRACTICES.

- CHOOSE EDUCATIONAL, INSPIRING, OR PROBLEM-SOLVING CONTENT FOR YOUR AUDIENCE

3. HOOK CREATION

- START OFF WITH A REFLECTIVE QUESTION OR A MEANINGFUL QUOTE THAT DRAWS PEOPLE INTO YOUR POST
("EVER KNOW HOW AYURVEDIC HABITS CAN AMAZINGLY CHANGE YOUR HEALTH?").

- WRITE HOOKS THAT CREATE THE URGE AND COMPEL THE READER TO DIG DEEPER.

4. SHARE CLEAR, ACTIONABLE VALUE

• BITE-SIZED: ENSURE EACH POST IN THE THREAD IS CONCISE AND STRAIGHTFORWARD.

ACTION ITEMS: DELIVER FOLLOWERS PRACTICAL AND ACTIONABLE GUIDANCE THEY CAN APPLY NOW.

USE LISTS AND STEPS BREAK BIG IDEAS INTO SIMPLE, EASY-TO-FOLLOW BULLET POINTS OR NUMBERED LISTS.

5. USE IMAGES

• USE HIGH-QUALITY IMAGES OR INFOGRAPHICS THAT ENFORCE THE MESSAGE.

• USE SHORT VIDEOS OR CAROUSEL POSTS FOR PROVIDING RICHER CONTENT.

6. USE INTERACTIVE ELEMENTS

• END YOUR THREADS WITH CTAS.

- ASK THE READERS TO COMMENT THEIR EXPERIENCES OR SHARE THE THREAD.

• USE INTERACTIVE QUESTIONS (SUCH AS "WHICH OF THESE HERBS DO YOU USE DAILY?") FOR MORE ENGAGEMENT.

7. KEEP IT CONSISTENT AND AUTHENTIC

• REGULAR POSTS WILL KEEP YOUR AUDIENCE ENGAGED AND MAKE A CONNECTION.

• STICK TO YOUR VOICE AND BRAND MESSAGE TO KEEP PEOPLE TRUSTING YOU.

8. CLOSE WITH A PUNCH

• TAKEAWAY: SUMMARIZE THE MAIN TAKEAWAYS, OR LEAVE THEM WITH ONE LAST PIECE OF ADVICE.

• END IT WITH A CTA SUCH AS "FOLLOW FOR MORE WELLNESS TIPS!" OR "SHARE THIS THREAD IF YOU FOUND IT USEFUL."

9. DEVIATION AND EDITING

• MONITOR ENGAGEMENT METRICS, WHICH COULD BE LIKES, SHARES, AND COMMENTS ON POSTS, TO KNOW THE MOST RELATABLE CONTENT.

• EMPLOY THOSE INSIGHTS TO UPDATE THE CONTENT IN THE FUTURE WITH THE AIM OF PERFORMING BETTER.

EXAMPLE THREAD STRUCTURE:

POST 1:

"ARE YOU HAVING TROUBLE FINDING NATURAL WAYS TO BOOST YOUR ENERGY? HERE'S HOW AYURVEDIC PRACTICES CAN HELP! [THREAD]"

POST 2-6:

ELABORATE ADVICE, DESCRIPTION, AND BENEFITS.

CONCLUSION:

"WHICH OF THESE TIPS WILL YOU TRY FIRST? LET US KNOW IN THE COMMENTS! DON'T FORGET TO FOLLOW FOR MORE NATURAL WELLNESS TIPS."

THROUGH ALL THE STEPS MENTIONED EARLIER, YOU CAN CREATE ENGAGING, VALUE-PACKED CONTENT THAT INSPIRES A LOYAL COMMUNITY AND DRIVES YOUR AUDIENCE ON INSTAGRAM THREADS TO ENGAGE EFFECTIVELY.

OVER ALL SUMMARY: CREATE VALUE-DRIVEN CONTENT:

- EDUCATIONAL POSTS: SHARE TIPS, HOW-TO GUIDES, OR INDUSTRY INSIGHTS RELEVANT TO YOUR AUDIENCE.

- STORYTELLING: USE MULTIPLE POSTS IN A THREAD TO TELL A COMPELLING STORY THAT RESONATES EMOTIONALLY WITH YOUR AUDIENCE.

- BEHIND-THE-SCENES: PROVIDE A GLIMPSE INTO YOUR PROCESS, TEAM, OR THE MAKING OF YOUR PRODUCT/SERVICE.

ENGAGE WITH INTERACTIVE ELEMENTS

ENGAGE WITH INTERACTIVE ELEMENTS TO INCREASE YOUR POST VIEWS AND COMMUNITY ENGAGEMENT. HERE'S HOW YOU CAN USE THE INTERACTIVE FEATURES OF AN INSTAGRAM THREAD TO YOUR BEST ADVANTAGE:

1. ASK QUESTIONS THAT HELP ELICIT A RESPONSE

YOU COULD END OR BEGIN YOUR INSTAGRAM THREADS WITH A QUESTION THAT WILL PROVOKE A RESPONSE.

HERE ARE SOME IDEAS:
"WHICH OF YOUR FAVORITE AYURVEDIC HERBS IS THIS, AND WHY?" OR "HOW HAVE YOU EVER USED HERBAL REMEDIES IN YOUR EVERYDAY LIFE?"

ALWAYS PHRASE YOUR QUESTIONS AS SPECIFIC AS POSSIBLE TO HELP ELICIT A RESPONSE.

EXAMPLE:
"HAVE YOU EVER TRIED GOLDEN MILK FOR ITS HEALTH BENEFITS?"

2. USE POLLS AND QUIZZES

- YOU CANNOT MAKE A POLL INSIDE THREADS. HOWEVER, YOU CAN COME UP WITH A THREAD THAT SOMEWHAT MIMICS A POLL BY ASKING USERS TO COMMENT ON THEIR CHOICES.

FOR EXAMPLE:

"COMMENT WITH A LEAF? FOR TULSI OR WITH A FLOWER? FOR TURMERIC".

FLICKER ASKING YOUR FOLLOWERS TO GUESS A MINI-QUIZ THREAD WITH SOME INFORMATION YOU'RE SHARING.

3. ADD CTAS

- CTAS SHOULD REMIND YOUR AUDIENCE OF WHAT TO DO NEXT.

YOU MIGHT FIND SUCH AS:

"DOUBLE-TAP IF YOU LOVE NATURAL REMEDIES!"

"TAG A FRIEND WHO NEEDS TO TRY THESE HERBAL TIPS!"

"SAVE THIS THREAD FOR WHEN YOU NEED QUICK AYURVEDIC TIPS!"

END YOUR POSTS WITH AN INVITATION TO SHARE THEIR THOUGHTS:

"HAVE YOU EXPERIENCED THE BENEFITS OF ASHWAGANDHA? SHARE YOUR STORY BELOW!"

4. INVITE USER-GENERATED CONTENT

- ASK TO SHARE THEIR EXPERIENCES BY ASKING THEM TO COMMENT WITH THEIR ROUTINES OR RESULTS
I.E., "TRIED ANY OF THESE RECIPES? SHARE YOUR RESULTS IN THE COMMENTS!"

- EASY CHALLENGE/CAMPAIGN WHERE USERS WILL CREATE POSTS AND TAG YOUR ACCOUNT.

5. VISUAL CLUES AND EMOJIS

- USE EMOJIS FOR ENGAGING AND EASY-TO-READ POSTS

EXAMPLE:

"WHAT'S YOUR GO-TO HERBAL TEA? 🍵 COMMENT BELOW!"

EXAMPLE:

ARROWS ( ) OR CHECKMARKS (■) ARE EXAMPLES OF EMOJIS THAT CAN INDICATE ACTION, LETTING READERS KNOW WHICH PARTS OF A THREAD TO FOCUS ON.

6. START THREADS THAT GENERATE DISCUSSIONS

SHARE LINKS, NEWS, OR POPULAR TOPICS IN YOUR NICHE. IF THERE IS BREAKING NEWS ABOUT A NEW BENEFIT OF AN HERB OR AN EMERGING AYURVEDIC TREND,

START THE DISCUSSION BY SHARING YOUR TAKE AND ASKING OTHERS FOR THEIRS.

ASK FOR DEBATE OR OPINION-FORUM THREADS, LIKE

"SOME BELIEVE THAT AYURVEDA IS THE WAY FORWARD TO MODERN HEALTH, BUT OTHERS ARE MORE SKEPTICAL. WHAT'S YOUR TAKE ON THIS?"

7. BRING COMMENTS TO THE FOREFRONT

• INVOLVE YOUR AUDIENCE BY COMMENTING ON THEIR COMMENTS, AND BRING ATTENTION TO THOUGHTFUL OR INFORMATIVE RESPONSES IN SUBSEQUENT POSTS OR STORIES.

THE PUBLIC IS EVEN MORE LIKELY TO WEIGH IN BECAUSE THEY KNOW SOMEONE'S COMMENTS WILL BE NOTICED AND APPRECIATED.

LIKE IMPORTANT OR ENGAGING COMMENTS IF POSSIBLE SINCE IT BRINGS ATTENTION TO USER INTERACTION.

8. CHALLENGES AND HASHTAGS

MAKE A CHALLENGE THREAD WHERE YOUR FOLLOWERS CAN PARTICIPATE WITH A UNIQUE HASHTAG (FOR INSTANCE, #HERBALHEALINGCHALLENGE).

INSTRUCT USERS TO SHARE THEIR CONTENT USING THE HASHTAG AS WELL AS TAG YOUR ACCOUNT

ACTIVE THREAD EXAMPLE

POST 1: "STRESS? 5 AYURVEDIC WAYS TO CALM DOWN [THREAD]"

POST 2-5: EXPAND ON EACH ONE OF THE PRACTICES.

FINAL POST:

"WHICH PRACTICE DO YOU ALREADY DO, OR WHICH ONE ARE YOU EXCITED TO TRY? LET US KNOW IN THE COMMENTS!? #NATURALCALM"

THESE INTERACTIVE ELEMENTS WILL BUILD A BETTER AND MORE INTIMATE RELATIONSHIP BETWEEN YOUR AUDIENCE AND YOUR CONTENT ON INSTAGRAM THREADS.

OVER ALL SUMMARY: ENGAGE WITH INTERACTIVE ELEMENTS:

- QUESTIONS AND POLLS: ADD INTERACTIVE PROMPTS IN YOUR THREADS TO ENCOURAGE PARTICIPATION.

- CALL-TO-ACTION (CTA): END YOUR THREAD WITH A CTA ASKING READERS TO COMMENT, SHARE, OR VISIT YOUR PROFILE FOR MORE INFORMATION.

CONSISTENT POSTING SCHEDULE

REFERS TO UPLOADING CONTENT AT REGULAR TIMES IN A STRATEGIC MANNER TO KEEP THE AUDIENCE INVOLVED AND VISIBLE.

CONSISTENCY IN POSTING BRINGS TRUST, KEEPS THE AUDIENCE HOOKED ONTO THE CONTENT, AND INFORMS INSTAGRAM'S ALGORITHM THAT ONE'S CONTENT IS WORTHY ENOUGH TO HAVE A BETTER REACH.

HOW TO MAINTAIN CONSISTENT POSTING SCHEDULE ON THREADS IN INSTAGRAM?

WHEN TO POST

- **PEAK TIMES ANALYSIS:**

USE INSTAGRAM ANALYTICS TO BE AWARE OF WHEN YOUR AUDIENCE IS MOST ACTIVE. IN THIS WAY, YOU GET TO KNOW WHEN TO SHARE YOUR CONTENT SO THAT USERS ARE LIKELY TO ENGAGE.

- **BROAD BEST TIMES:**

WHILE SCIENTIFIC EVIDENCE POINTS TO MID-MORNINGS (9-11 A.M.) AND EARLY EVENINGS (7-9 P.M.) THROUGHOUT THE WEEK AS THE "BEST" TIMES OF THE DAY, IT DOES VARY WIDELY BY NICHE AND AUDIENCE LOCATION.

- **TEST AND ADJUST:**

POST AT DIFFERENT TIMES AND MEASURE YOUR ENGAGEMENT.

THIS WILL HELP GUIDE YOU TO THE BEST TIME SLOTS THAT WORK EFFECTIVELY FOR YOUR AUDIENCE.

2. WHAT TO POST

- **VALUE-DRIVEN CONTENT:**

ENSURE THAT THE CONTENT YOU HAVE IS A VALUE PROPOSITION IN ITSELF, WHETHER THROUGH EDUCATIONAL TIPS, BEHIND-THE-SCENES MOMENTS, OR USER-GENERATED STORIES.

FOR EXAMPLE:

WHEN IT COMES TO THE NICHE OF HERBAL AND AYURVEDA, POST ON HOW HERBS WILL BENEFIT A PARTICULAR BODY OR DAILY WELLNESS PRACTICES, INCLUDING DIY HERBAL RECIPES.

·**INTERACTIVE THREADS:**

TRY TO COME UP WITH POST IDEAS THAT WILL INVITE PEOPLE TO COMMENT, SHARE, OR ENGAGE WITH YOUR BRAND. USE QUESTIONS, POLLS, AND CHALLENGES TO GET THE AUDIENCE TALKING.

· **MIX CONTENT TYPES:**
VARY AMONG KINDS OF CONTENTS LIKE TIPS, PERSONAL STORIES, INFOGRAPHICS, AND VIDEOS. IT KEEPS YOUR PROFILE INTERESTING AND DYNAMIC.

· **SEASONAL AND TRENDING TOPICS:**

IDENTIFY RELEVANT TRENDS AND SEASONAL TOPICS SO YOU'LL ALWAYS STAY UPDATED. FOR EXAMPLE, SUGGEST VARIOUS HERBAL DRINKS THAT CAN BOOST IMMUNITY DURING FLU SEASON.

3. WHY TO POST

• MORE ENGAGEMENT:

WITH CONSISTENT POSTS, YOUR CONTENT GETS DISPLAYED MORE FREQUENTLY IN THE FOLLOWERS' FEEDS, AND THEY ARE SUGGESTED TO OTHER PEOPLE ALSO.

• TRUST AMONG THE AUDIENCE:

CONSISTENCY SHOWS YOU ARE ACTIVE AND SERIOUS ABOUT THE CONTENT YOU ARE POSTING. THIS WILL ENSURE A SENSE OF TRUST AMONG YOUR AUDIENCE AND CONSIDER YOU AS A SOURCE OF INFORMATION THAT IS RELIABLE.

• CREATES THE HABIT OF ENGAGEMENT:

BECAUSE YOU POST REGULARLY, YOUR AUDIENCE BEGINS TO EXPECT YOUR POSTS AND BECOMES ACCUSTOMED TO ENGAGING WITH YOUR POSTS.

- **PROMOTES ALGORITHM FRIENDLINESS:**

SINCE THE INSTAGRAM ALGORITHM FAVORS ACCOUNTS THAT ARE POSTING RELENTLESSLY AND INTERACT WITH THEIR AUDIENCE, IT CAN TRANSLATE TO MORE FREQUENT APPEARANCES OF YOUR POSTS ON THE EXPLORE PAGE OR IN OTHER USERS' FEEDS.

USE THESE TIPS TO KEEP POSTING REGULARLY

. **PLAN AHEAD:**

HAVE A CONTENT CALENDAR OR SCHEDULING TOOL TO CREATE POSTS, MEANING YOU'LL NEVER FORGET YOUR BEST POSTING TIMES.

- **SET REALISTIC GOALS:**
YOU MIGHT START BY POSTING A NUMBER OF TIMES THAT YOU'RE ABLE TO HOLD (EXAMPLE: 3-4 TIMES PER WEEK),

GOALS THEN INCREASE THE FREQUENCY AS YOU GET MORE COMFORTABLE.

. BATCH CONTENT CREATION:

CREATE MULTIPLE POSTS AT ONCE, SAVING TIME AND STREAMLINING YOUR PROCESS.

. INTERACTION AFTER POSTING:

ENSURE TO SPEND A MINIMUM OF 15-30 MINUTES ENGAGING WITH COMMENTS AND INTERACTION WITH OTHER POSTS IN THE THREADS AFTER POSTING FOR OPTIMAL VISIBILITY AND ENGAGEMENT.

EXAMPLE :

HERBAL AND AYURVEDA CONTENT CALENDAR SAMPLE

• MONDAY:

WELLNESS TIP KICK-STARTER OF THE WEEK (FOR EXAMPLE, AN ADVANTAGE OF HAVING A MORNING RITUAL WITH LEMON WATER).

- **WEDNESDAY:**

EDUCATIONAL POST ABOUT A GIVEN HERB AND ITS USES; USE THESE TYPES OF TITLES: "ASHWAGANDHA: THE SECRET TO REDUCING STRESS").

- **FRIDAY:**

INTERACTIVITY (QUESTION OR SURVEY) ("WHICH OF THE FOLLOWING HERBAL BEVERAGES DO YOU LIKE TO USE FOR UNWINDING: CHAMOMILE TEA OR GOLDEN MILK?").

- **SUNDAY:**

PERSONAL STORY OR COMMUNITY SPOTLIGHT ("HOW EMBRACING AYURVEDA LIFESTYLE PRACTICES TRANSFORMED MY LIFE—SHARE YOURS BELOW!").

CONCLUSION

THIS WILL HELP MAINTAIN A CONSISTENT POSTING SCHEDULE ON INSTAGRAM THREADS SO THAT FOLLOWERS KNOW WHEN TO EXPECT CONTENT FROM YOU. IT ALSO ESTABLISHES YOUR PRESENCE IN YOUR NICHE AND CAN REALLY HELP BOOST ENGAGEMENT.

SO FOCUS ON BALANCED MIX CONTENT TYPES THAT ARE VALUABLE, INTERACTIVE, AND TIMED RIGHT TO KEEP YOUR AUDIENCE ENGAGED AND YOUR PROFILE GROWING.

OVER ALL SUMMARY : CONSISTENT POSTING SCHEDULE

- REGULARLY POST THREADS TO KEEP YOUR AUDIENCE ENGAGED AND COMING BACK FOR MORE.

- USE A MIX OF LONG-FORM AND SHORTER, SNAPPY POSTS TO MAINTAIN VARIETY.

LEVERAGE VISUALS

LEVERAGING VISUALS EFFECTIVELY ON THREADS (INSTAGRAM'S TEXT-BASED PLATFORM) IS A BIT OF A CREATIVE CHALLENGE BECAUSE THE PLATFORM IS PRIMARILY FOCUSED ON TEXT.

HOWEVER, YOU CAN STILL INTEGRATE VISUAL ELEMENTS LIKE IMAGES, VIDEOS, MEMES, AND INFOGRAPHICS INTO YOUR THREADS TO ENHANCE ENGAGEMENT AND CAPTURE ATTENTION.

BELOW ARE STRATEGIES FOR INCORPORATING VISUALS IN YOUR THREADS POSTS, WITH REAL-WORLD EXAMPLES AND CASE STUDIES TO GUIDE YOU.

1. USE IMAGES TO ENHANCE TEXTUAL CONTENT

WHILE THREADS IS TEXT-FOCUSED, YOU CAN USE COMPELLING IMAGES TO COMPLEMENT YOUR WORDS AND BREAK UP THE TEXT. A POWERFUL IMAGE OR PHOTO CAN MAKE YOUR POST MORE EYE-CATCHING, ENCOURAGE ENGAGEMENT, AND GIVE CONTEXT TO YOUR MESSAGE.

EXAMPLE: NIKE
NIKE OFTEN PAIRS THEIR MOTIVATIONAL TEXT WITH POWERFUL IMAGES OF ATHLETES OR THEIR PRODUCTS IN ACTION. THE IMAGES AMPLIFY THEIR MESSAGE AND INSPIRE FOLLOWERS TO TAKE ACTION, WHETHER IT'S EXERCISING OR BUYING THEIR PRODUCTS.

- STRATEGY: USE HIGH-QUALITY, RELEVANT IMAGES THAT SUPPORT THE MESSAGE OF YOUR POST. THIS COULD BE ANYTHING FROM PRODUCT PHOTOS TO LIFESTYLE SHOTS THAT ALIGN WITH YOUR BRAND.

- TAKEAWAY: ADDING STRONG, RELEVANT IMAGERY INCREASES THE VISUAL APPEAL AND ENGAGEMENT OF YOUR THREADS.

2. CREATE VISUAL QUOTES OR TEXT OVERLAYS

ANOTHER WAY TO INTEGRATE VISUALS INTO YOUR THREADS IS BY USING QUOTE GRAPHICS OR TEXT OVERLAYS. YOU CAN DESIGN A SIMPLE YET IMPACTFUL IMAGE THAT FEATURES AN INSPIRATIONAL QUOTE OR A KEY MESSAGE, OVERLAID ON A VISUALLY APPEALING BACKGROUND.

EXAMPLE: CANVA
CANVA IS A GREAT EXAMPLE OF A BRAND THAT USES QUOTE GRAPHICS TO INCREASE ENGAGEMENT. THEY REGULARLY POST VISUALLY COMPELLING IMAGES THAT FEATURE DESIGN TIPS, MOTIVATIONAL QUOTES, OR USER-GENERATED CONTENT IN A STYLIZED FORMAT, MAKING THE TEXT BOTH DIGESTIBLE AND SHAREABLE.

- **STRATEGY:** USE APPS LIKE CANVA OR ADOBE SPARK TO CREATE EYE-CATCHING GRAPHICS THAT COMBINE YOUR MESSAGE WITH BEAUTIFUL BACKGROUNDS AND TYPOGRAPHY.
- **TAKEAWAY:** VISUALS PAIRED WITH TEXT CAN MAKE YOUR POSTS MORE ENGAGING AND LIKELY TO BE SHARED

3. INCORPORATE MEMES AND GIFS

MEMES AND GIFS ARE EXTREMELY SHAREABLE AND CAN QUICKLY GO VIRAL. THREADS CAN BENEFIT FROM USING VISUAL HUMOR, AND THESE CAN SIGNIFICANTLY ENHANCE THE VIRALITY OF YOUR CONTENT.

EXAMPLE: WENDY'S TWITTER ROASTS

WENDY'S TWITTER ACCOUNT IS FAMOUS FOR ITS WITTY, MEME-DRIVEN CONTENT THAT GOES VIRAL DUE TO THE HUMOROUS USE OF GIFS, MEMES, AND VISUAL JOKES. THEY OFTEN SHARE HUMOROUS VISUALS IN RESPONSE TO CUSTOMER INQUIRIES, WHICH INCREASES ENGAGEMENT AND SHARES.

- **STRATEGY:** USE MEMES OR RELEVANT GIFS TO MAKE YOUR POSTS HUMOROUS, RELATABLE, OR TOPICAL.

- **TAKEAWAY:** MEMES AND GIFS HUMANIZE YOUR BRAND AND MAKE YOUR POSTS MORE RELATABLE, INCREASING THE CHANCES OF GOING VIRAL.

4. USE CAROUSEL OR MULTIPLE IMAGES

WHILE THREADS IS NOT INHERENTLY BUILT FOR CAROUSELS, YOU CAN STILL POST MULTIPLE IMAGES IN ONE THREAD TO TELL A STORY OR SHARE A SEQUENCE OF VISUALS. THIS CAN INCLUDE BEFORE-AND-AFTER PHOTOS, PRODUCT FEATURES, OR SEQUENTIAL STORYTELLING.

CASE STUDY: NATIONAL GEOGRAPHIC

NATIONAL GEOGRAPHIC OFTEN SHARES MULTIPLE STUNNING IMAGES IN THEIR POSTS. THESE IMAGES ARE RELATED TO WILDLIFE, LANDSCAPES, OR CULTURAL SUBJECTS AND ENHANCE THEIR STORYTELLING, MAKING IT MORE ENGAGING.

- **STRATEGY**: POST MULTIPLE IMAGES IN A THREAD THAT BUILDS ON A NARRATIVE OR OFFERS DETAILED INSIGHT INTO YOUR TOPIC.
- **TAKEAWAY:** MULTIPLE IMAGES IN A THREAD CAN MAKE YOUR POST MORE IMMERSIVE AND ENGAGING, ENCOURAGING USERS TO SWIPE THROUGH.

5. LEVERAGE INTERACTIVE VISUALS (POLLS, QUIZZES, & QUESTIONS)

INCORPORATING INTERACTIVE VISUALS INTO YOUR THREADS CAN BOOST ENGAGEMENT BY ENCOURAGING FOLLOWERS TO ACTIVELY PARTICIPATE IN THE CONVERSATION. INSTAGRAM'S STORIES OFTEN USE THESE FEATURES, BUT YOU CAN REPLICATE THEM ON THREADS USING VISUAL PROMPTS.

EXAMPLE: STARBUCKS

STARBUCKS USES INTERACTIVE POSTS THAT ASK QUESTIONS, ENCOURAGE PEOPLE TO SHARE THEIR FAVORITE DRINK, OR TAKE PART IN A POLL. WHILE THIS FEATURE IS MORE COMMONLY SEEN IN STORIES, YOU CAN PROMPT THE SAME LEVEL OF INTERACTION THROUGH YOUR VISUALS IN THREADS.

- **STRATEGY:** CREATE VISUAL PROMPTS THAT ASK QUESTIONS, CREATE A CALL TO ACTION, OR ASK FOR FEEDBACK FROM YOUR FOLLOWERS.

- **TAKEAWAY:** INTERACTIVE VISUALS INCREASE USER INVOLVEMENT AND CAN SPARK CONVERSATIONS THAT MAKE YOUR POSTS MORE ENGAGING.

6. LEVERAGE AR FILTERS OR VIRTUAL TRY-ONS

IF YOU'RE IN AN INDUSTRY THAT CAN BENEFIT FROM IT, USING AUGMENTED REALITY (AR) CAN ENHANCE YOUR THREADS BY ALLOWING USERS TO INTERACT WITH THE POST IN A FUN AND INNOVATIVE WAY. INSTAGRAM OFFERS AR FILTERS THAT YOU CAN ENCOURAGE YOUR AUDIENCE TO USE.

EXAMPLE: GUCCI

GUCCI USED INSTAGRAM'S AR FILTERS TO CREATE VIRTUAL TRY-ONS FOR THEIR SNEAKERS, ALLOWING USERS TO "TRY" THE SHOES ON BY UPLOADING THEIR OWN IMAGES OR VIDEOS. THIS INNOVATION DROVE INTERACTION AND SHAREABILITY.

- **STRATEGY:** IF APPLICABLE, CREATE AR FILTERS THAT ALLOW USERS TO ENGAGE WITH YOUR BRAND IN A VIRTUAL SPACE (LIKE TRYING ON PRODUCTS OR EXPLORING A PRODUCT'S FEATURES).

- **TAKEAWAY:** AR CAN INCREASE INTERACTION AND ENGAGEMENT, LEADING TO MORE VISIBILITY AND VIRAL POTENTIAL.

7. INFOGRAPHICS AND DATA VISUALIZATION

INFOGRAPHICS AND DATA-DRIVEN CONTENT CAN BE SHARED ON THREADS, ESPECIALLY WHEN YOU WANT TO HIGHLIGHT KEY STATISTICS, FACTS, OR TRENDS. USE CLEAN AND SIMPLE VISUALIZATIONS TO SUPPORT THE MESSAGE OF YOUR POST.

EXAMPLE: HUBSPOT

HUBSPOT REGULARLY SHARES INFOGRAPHICS THAT DISTILL COMPLEX MARKETING DATA INTO EASY-TO-READ, SHAREABLE VISUALS. THESE GRAPHICS BREAK DOWN KEY STATISTICS, TRENDS, OR PROCESSES IN A WAY THAT'S VISUALLY ENGAGING.

- **STRATEGY**: IF YOU HAVE DATA OR INSIGHTS TO SHARE, CREATE VISUALLY APPEALING INFOGRAPHICS TO ACCOMPANY YOUR THREADS. USE SIMPLE CHARTS, ICONS, AND TYPOGRAPHY TO MAKE THE CONTENT DIGESTIBLE.

- **TAKEAWAY**: INFOGRAPHICS SIMPLIFY COMPLEX INFORMATION AND MAKE YOUR POSTS MORE ENGAGING, ENCOURAGING SHARES AND DISCUSSIONS.

8. BEHIND-THE-SCENES VISUALS

SHOWING BEHIND-THE-SCENES CONTENT HELPS HUMANIZE YOUR BRAND AND BUILDS A CONNECTION WITH YOUR AUDIENCE. THIS KIND OF CONTENT IS OFTEN VISUALLY APPEALING BECAUSE IT'S MORE AUTHENTIC AND RELATABLE.

EXAMPLE: COCA-COLA

COCA-COLA SHARES BEHIND-THE-SCENES VISUALS OF THEIR PRODUCTION PROCESS, COMMUNITY EVENTS, AND WORKPLACE CULTURE. THIS APPROACH BUILDS A NARRATIVE AROUND THEIR BRAND THAT IS PERSONAL AND RELATABLE.

- **STRATEGY:** SHARE BEHIND-THE-SCENES CONTENT USING CASUAL, AUTHENTIC VISUALS THAT TELL THE STORY OF YOUR BRAND AND PEOPLE.

- **TAKEAWAY**: BEHIND-THE-SCENES CONTENT CREATES A STRONGER CONNECTION WITH YOUR AUDIENCE, MAKING YOUR BRAND MORE RELATABLE.

9. CREATE VISUAL CAMPAIGNS

LAUNCH A CAMPAIGN WITH A CONSISTENT VISUAL THEME THAT CAN BE SHARED ACROSS MULTIPLE POSTS IN YOUR THREADS. THIS WILL HELP REINFORCE YOUR MESSAGE AND CREATE A SENSE OF ANTICIPATION AND ENGAGEMENT.

EXAMPLE: NIKE'S #JUSTDOIT CAMPAIGN

NIKE'S #JUSTDOIT CAMPAIGN IS A PRIME EXAMPLE OF A VISUAL CAMPAIGN THAT THREADS ITS WAY THROUGH ALL THEIR SOCIAL MEDIA CONTENT, INCLUDING IMAGES, TEXT, AND VIDEOS. THE CONSISTENCY OF THE VISUAL THEME REINFORCES THE MESSAGE AND ENGAGES USERS.

- **STRATEGY**: DEVELOP A CAMPAIGN WITH A CONSISTENT VISUAL THEME AND ASK FOLLOWERS TO PARTICIPATE BY SHARING THEIR OWN RELATED CONTENT.

- **TAKEAWAY:** CONSISTENT VISUAL CAMPAIGNS BUILD BRAND RECOGNITION AND ENGAGE AUDIENCES OVER TIME.

10. USE TIMELY AND TREND-BASED VISUALS

TIMELY VISUALS, ESPECIALLY THOSE THAT TAP INTO CURRENT TRENDS OR VIRAL MOMENTS, CAN GREATLY ENHANCE YOUR THREADS' VIRALITY. WHETHER IT'S A HOLIDAY, TRENDING MEME, OR EVENT, RELEVANT VISUALS MAKE YOUR POSTS MORE TIMELY AND SHAREABLE.

EXAMPLE: MCDONALD'S SEASONAL CAMPAIGNS

MCDONALD'S OFTEN USES SEASONALLY THEMED VISUALS, SUCH AS HOLIDAY-THEMED MEALS OR LIMITED EDITION PRODUCTS. THESE VISUALS TAP INTO THE EXCITEMENT AROUND SPECIAL EVENTS, MAKING THE CONTENT MORE RELEVANT AND LIKELY TO GO VIRAL.

- **STRATEGY:** CREATE VISUALS TIED TO CURRENT EVENTS, HOLIDAYS, OR TRENDING TOPICS TO MAKE YOUR CONTENT FEEL TIMELY AND RELEVANT.

- **TAKEAWAY:** TIMELY AND TREND-BASED VISUALS CREATE URGENCY AND RELEVANCE, WHICH DRIVES ENGAGEMENT AND SHARING.

CONCLUSION:

EVEN THOUGH THREADS IS PRIMARILY A TEXT-BASED PLATFORM, YOU CAN STILL EFFECTIVELY LEVERAGE VISUALS TO ENHANCE YOUR POSTS, INCREASE ENGAGEMENT, AND OPTIMIZE FOR VIRALITY.

BY INCORPORATING HIGH-QUALITY IMAGES, MEMES, INFOGRAPHICS, INTERACTIVE VISUALS, AR, AND BEHIND-THE-SCENES CONTENT, YOU CAN CRAFT COMPELLING POSTS THAT RESONATE WITH YOUR AUDIENCE AND DRIVE HIGHER ENGAGEMENT.

THE KEY IS TO CREATE A SEAMLESS INTEGRATION OF TEXT AND VISUALS THAT NOT ONLY CAPTURES ATTENTION BUT ALSO ADDS VALUE TO YOUR FOLLOWERS.

OVER ALL SUMMARY: LEVERAGE VISUALS:

- INCLUDE HIGH-QUALITY IMAGES: USE VISUALLY APPEALING PHOTOS OR GRAPHICS TO BREAK UP TEXT AND KEEP READERS INTERESTED.

- USE VIDEOS: SHORT VIDEOS THAT ADD DEPTH TO YOUR CONTENT CAN BOOST ENGAGEMENT SIGNIFICANTLY.

OPTIMIZE FOR VIRALITY

POST OPTIMIZATION ON THREADS (AN INSTAGRAM TEXT-BASED PLATFORM) FOR VIRALITY INVOLVES USING STRATEGIES THAT INCREASE VIEWS, ENGAGEMENT, AND SHARING. FOLLOW ME BELOW AS I DETAIL THE STRATEGIES YOU CAN USE FOR OPTIMIZING YOUR POSTS, COMPLEMENTED BY EXAMPLES AND CASE STUDIES OF HOW BRANDS AND INFLUENCERS HAVE ACHIEVED VIRALITY.

1. CRAFT COMPELLING, SHAREABLE CONTENT

- **HOOK**: THE WORDS OR PHRASES THAT INTRODUCE YOUR POST SHOULD BE ENGAGING ENOUGH TO GET USERS TO CONTINUE SCROLLING.

- **CONCISE & CREDIBILITY**: POSTS SHOULD BE SHORT BUT INFORMATIVE. VIRALITY COMMONLY FAVORS SHORT INFORMATION THAT IS EASY TO CONSUME.

- **EMOTIONAL CONNECTION**: POSTS THAT BRING EMOTIONS (LAUGHTER, AMAZEMENT, CURIOSITY) NORMALLY GAIN MORE SHARES.

EXAMPLE :

WENDY'S TWITTER ROASTS

WENDY'S TWITTER ACCOUNT IS KNOWN BY ITS ROASTING, HUMOROUS TWEETS,FOR AND ROASTS. GENERALLY, SUCH POSTS ARE VIRAL BECAUSE THEY BRING OUT LAUGHTER AND SURPRISES, HENCE MAKING PEOPLE SHARE THEM.

• **TACTIC:** USE HUMOR, TRENDING TOPICS, OR BOLD STATEMENTS TO CREATE POSTS THAT ARE IMPOSSIBLE TO IGNORE.

•**INSIGHT:** POSTS THAT MAKE PEOPLE LAUGH OR GO INTO SHOCK ARE MORE LIKELY TO GET SHARED.

2. LEVERAGE TRENDING TOPICS AND HASHTAGS

- **LEVERAGE POPULAR HASHTAGS**: KEEP YOURSELF UPDATED BY INCLUDING TRENDING HASHTAGS IN YOUR THREADS. IT MAKES THEM MORE DISCOVERABLE TO THE USERS WHO FOLLOW OR SEARCH FOR THOSE HASHTAGS.

- **TAP INTO POP CULTURE & CURRENT EVENTS:** MAKE YOUR POST RELEVANT TO WHAT IS HAPPENING IN THE WORLD, WHETHER IT IS A TRENDING MEME, A GLOBAL EVENT, OR A HOT TOPIC.

- **TIMELINESS, ENGAGE IN REAL-TIME CONVERSATIONS:** BE TIMELY BY ENGAGING WITH CONVERSATIONS OVER WHAT'S TRENDING.

CASE STUDY: OREO'S "DUNK IN THE DARK" SUPER BOWL AD

OREO'S INFAMOUS "DUNK IN THE DARK" AD WENT VIRAL DURING THE 2013 SUPER BOWL BLACKOUT.
OREO USED THE UNEXPECTED MOMENT TO A GREAT ADVANTAGE BY POSTING A TIMELY AND RELEVANT VISUAL THAT RESONATED WITH PEOPLE AT THE MOMENT

- **STRATEGY:**

LEVERAGE REAL-TIME CONVERSATIONS. IDENTIFY CHANCES FOR UNFORESEEN EVENTS OR VIRAL MOMENTS TO ATTRACT ATTENTION THROUGH AN APPROPRIATE, TIMELY RESPONSE.

- **TAKEAWAY:**

TIMELINESS AND RELEVANCE CAN HELP A POST GO VIRAL FOR A BRAND.

3. CREATE CONTENT FOR ENGAGEMENT (POLLS, QUESTIONS, CONTESTS)

- **INDUCTIVE RESPONSES:**

POSTS THAT ASK PEOPLE TO GIVE RESPONSES IN THE FORM OF QUESTIONS, POLLS, OR THROUGH CALLS ARE MORE LIKELY TO GO VIRAL. THE MORE THE USERS RESPOND, THE HIGHER THE CHANCES OF GETTING YOUR POST VIEWED.

CONTESTS OR GIVEAWAYS:

THIS IS ONE OF THE AGE-OLD APPROACHES THROUGH WHICH CONTENT GOES VIRAL BY ASKING USERS TO LIKE OR SHARE TO WIN CONTESTS AND HENCE EXPANDS REACH.

EXAMPLE: NIKE'S "JUST DO IT" CHALLENGE

NIKE FREQUENTLY CONDUCTS VIRAL CAMPAIGNS BY ASKING USERS TO PARTICIPATE IN CHALLENGES OR EVEN CREATE THEIR OWN CONTENT RELATED TO THE CAMPAIGN. USERS WILL SHARE THEIR PERSONAL MOTIVATIONAL WORKOUT VIDEOS, THUS CREATING A HUGE ENGAGEMENT AND VIRALITY.

- **TACTIC:**

DESIGN A CAMPAIGN OR CHALLENGE THAT WILL ENCOURAGE YOUR AUDIENCE TO CREATE THEIR OWN CONTENT.

- **TAKEAWAY:**

THE ENGAGEMENT AS WELL AS THE VIRALITY STEM DIRECTLY FROM USER PARTICIPATION.

4. USE VISUALS AS ADDITIONAL INFORMATION TO ILLUSTRATE THE MESSAGE

· **INCORPORATE VISUAL GRAPHICS**: USE YOUR THREADS WITH HIGHER-QUALITY IMAGES OR SHORT VIDEO CLIPS, WHICH WOULD MAKE VIEWERS NOTICE YOUR POSTS MORE.

· **GIFS OR MEMES THAT PEOPLE WILL REMEMBER:**

ADDING MEMES OR GIFS TO YOUR CONTENT WILL MOST LIKELY GRAB SHARES AND INTERACTIONS, ESPECIALLY IF THEY ARE RELATED TO THE MOST POPULAR CULTURE OR HUMOR.

EXAMPLE: NETFLIX MEME MARKETING

MEME MARKETING IS DONE SO WELL BY NETFLIX IN RELATION TO FUNNY,

RELATABLE IMAGES THAT ARE SURE TO BE BOUND TO THOSE MOMENTS IN POP CULTURE ON TRENDS. MEMES ARE VERY SHAREABLE CONTENT, AND LOTS OF TIMES THEY GO VIRAL BECAUSE OF THEIR RELATEDNESS.

·

- **STRATEGY:**
USE MEMES OR VISUALS WITH YOUR TEXT TO AMPLIFY ENGAGEMENT.

- **TAKEAWAY:**

VISUAL CONTENT, ESPECIALLY MEMES, CAN POWER AMPLIFY SHAREABILITY AND VIRAL SPREAD.

5. INFLUENCER COLLABORATION

- **REACH INFLUENCER AUDIENCES:** THROUGH AN INFLUENCE RELATIONSHIP, YOU CAN TAP INTO THE INFLUENCER'S AUDIENCE BASED ON THEIR INFLUENCE ON YOUR CONTENT FOR A GREATER CHANCE OF VIEWS AND SHARES, ESPECIALLY IF THE INFLUENCER'S FOLLOWING MEANS SOMETHING TO YOUR TARGET AUDIENCE.

- **CO-CREATIVITY**: THROUGH INFLUENCERS OR OTHER BRANDS, CO-CREATE ENTERTAINING, INFORMING, OR INSPIRING CONTENT.

CASE STUDY: GYMSHARK AND FITNESS INFLUENCERS

THEIR PARTNERSHIPS WITH THE FITNESS INFLUENCERS HUGELY CONTRIBUTED TO VIRALITY. THEIR CAPABILITY OF USING THE INFLUENCERS BY SHARING WORKOUT VIDEOS AND TESTIMONIALS HELPED THEM REACH A HUGE AUDIENCE.

- **STRATEGY:** YOU CAN SPONSOR OR PARTNER WITH INFLUENCERS WHO RESONATE WITH YOUR BRAND VALUES AND TARGET AUDIENCE, WITH CONTENT THAT WILL HIT DEEPER INTO A BROADER AUDIENCE.

- **TAKEAWAY:** INFLUENCERS HELP AMPLIFY YOUR MESSAGE AND WILL, THEREFORE, MAKE YOUR POST REACH FURTHER.

6. POSTING CONSISTENTLY AND OPTIMIZING FOR TIMING

- **PEAK HOUR POSTING:** IDENTIFY THE HOUR OF DAY WHEN YOUR AUDIENCE IS MOST ACTIVE. POSTING DURING PEAK HOURS WILL INCREASE THE CHANCES THAT YOUR CAMPAIGN BECOMES VIRAL.

- CONSISTENCY IS THE KEY: POSTING REGULARLY CAN CREATE A CASCADE OF INTEREST AND KEEP THE AUDIENCE HANGING FOR YOUR POSTS.

EXAMPLE: STARBUCKS'S SEASONAL CONSISTENT POSTING

SEASONAL PROMOTIONS SUCH AS THE PSL GIVE STARBUCKS THE OPPORTUNITY TO PRODUCE POSTS THAT ALIGN WITH THE FEEL OF THE SEASON. ON A CONSISTENT BASIS, POSTING AGAINST THESE TRENDS KEEPS THEM IN PEOPLE'S MINDS.

- **STRATEGY:** POST OFTEN AND CONNECT YOUR CONTENT TO SOME SEASONAL EVENT OR TREND TO KEEP IT RELEVANT.

- **TAKEAWAY:** CONSISTENCY, COMBINED WITH SEASONALITY OR TRENDING TOPICS, KEEPS YOUR CONTENT VIEWED AND ENGAGED WITH.

7. CONTENT SPARKS DEBATE

CONTROVERSIAL OR THOUGHT-PROVOKING POSTS:

WHILE CONTROVERSIAL POSTS ARE A RISK, IT IS THE POSTS THAT QUESTION NORM OR PROVOKE DEBATE THAT END UP BEING SHARED AND COMMENTED ON, THUS ELEVATING THE ENGAGEMENT.

ASK THOUGHTFUL QUESTIONS:

THOUGHT-PROVOKING QUESTIONS MAKE PEOPLE THINK OR REFLECT ABOUT THEIR EXPERIENCES AND INCREASE THE CHANCES OF SHARING THAT POST

EXAMPLE: PATAGONIA'S ENVIRONMENTAL POSTS

PATAGONIA HAS LEVERAGED THE CORPORATION PLATFORM TO SHARE ENVIRONMENTAL THOUGHTS THAT ARE AS HEAVY IN DEBATE AND SHAREABILITY. USE YOUR PLATFORM BOLDLY TO INCITE AND MAKE CONVERSATION ACTION.

- **STRATEGY:** POST CONTENT THAT CHALLENGES THE IDEAS OR GETS PEOPLE TALKING, BUT ABSOLUTELY DON'T PUSH ACROSS BORDERS YOU DON'T WANT TO TREAD ON IN A WAY THAT DAMAGES YOUR BRAND.

- **TAKEAWAY:** THOUGHT-PROVOKING AND DISCUSSION-WORTHY POSTS STAND MORE OF A CHANCE TO GO VIRAL BECAUSE THEY GET SHARED WITH PERSONAL NETWORKS.

8. SOCIAL SHARING AND TAGGING

- **ASK FOLLOWERS TO SHARE OR TAG:**

CONTENT IS REQUESTED TO BE SHARED OR TAGGED THROUGH DIRECT CONTACT WITH YOUR FOLLOWERS BY ASKING THEM TO TAG FRIENDS OR POST IF THEY FIND IT INTERESTING OR RELATABLE.

- **DISTRIBUTABLE FORMATS:**

GIVETAG THE FOLLOWERS SOMETHING THEY WOULD WANT TO SHARE, SUCH AS VALUABLE ADVICE, INSPIRING QUOTES, OR ENTERTAINING CONTENT.

EXAMPLE: SHARE A COKE CAMPAIGN BY COCA-COLA

THE COCA-COLA "SHARE A COKE" CAMPAIGN ENCOURAGED PEOPLE TO BUY BOTTLES FEATURING THEIR NAMES AND GO ONLINE TO SHARE PICTURES, THUS CREATING A VIRAL MOVEMENT IN USER-GENERATED CONTENT.

•**TACTIC:** MAKE IT SHAREABLE AND CHALLENGE YOUR FOLLOWERS TO TAG THEIR FRIENDS.

TAKEAWAY: POSTING CONTENT THAT DIRECTLY ASKS FOR SHARING OR TAGGING INCREASES THE CHANCES OF YOUR CONTENT GOING VIRAL.

CONCLUSION:

FOR VIRALITY ON THREADS, YOU NEED TIMELY, EMOTIVE, ENGAGING, AND SHAREABLE CONTENT. TRENDS, USE OF HUMOR, VISUALS, AND COLLABORATION WITH INFLUENCERS CAN INCREASE YOUR CHANCES OF SUCCESS. YOU ALSO INCREASE THE REACH OF YOUR CONTENT IF YOU DO IT REGULARLY AND DURING STRATEGIC MOMENTS, ASSOCIATING IT WITH SOME INFLUENCER.

IN A COMPETITIVE SCENARIO, YOU MAXIMIZE YOUR POTENTIAL TO GO VIRAL WHEN YOU CREATE POSTS THAT COULD REALLY SPEAK TO THE HEARTS OF YOUR TARGET AUDIENCE AND GET THEM TO INTERACT WITH THE PIECE.

OVER ALL SUMMARY : OPTIMIZE FOR VIRALITY

- **HOOK AT THE START**: START EACH THREAD WITH A CAPTIVATING STATEMENT OR QUESTION TO GRAB ATTENTION.

- **EASY-TO-SHARE CONTENT**: CRAFT CONTENT THAT IS RELATABLE AND EASY FOR OTHERS TO SHARE WITH THEIR FOLLOWERS.

ANALYZE AND REFINE

ANALYZING AND REFINING YOUR THREADS ON INSTAGRAM IS THE KEY TO MAXIMIZING ENGAGEMENT AND ENSURING THAT YOUR CONTENT IS GOING TO RESONATE WITH YOUR AUDIENCE.

YOU HAVE TO ALWAYS BE REVIEWING, DEVELOPING INSIGHTS, AND MAKING DATA-DRIVEN DECISIONS TO MAKE YOUR POSTS STRONGER OVER TIME.

HERE ARE STRATEGIES FOR ANALYZING AND REFINING YOUR THREADS, COMPLETE WITH REAL-WORLD EXAMPLES AND CASE STUDIES TO ILLUSTRATE HOW THIS PROCESS WORKS.

1. TRACK ENGAGEMENT METRICS

START WITH MONITORING SOME KEY ENGAGEMENT METRICS TO GET AN UNDERSTANDING OF HOW YOUR THREADS ARE DOING. IN TERMS OF:

- **LIKES:** THE NUMBER OF PEOPLE LIKING YOUR POST. IT'S JUST THE MOST SIMPLISTIC ENGAGEMENT METRIC.

- **COMMENTS:** THE AMOUNT OF DISCUSSION OR INTERACTION HAPPENING WITH YOUR CONTENT

- **SHARES:** IF YOUR POST IS SHARED, THEN THERE IS A POTENTIAL FOR VIRALITY. MOST SHARED CONTENT TENDS TO GO VIRAL.

- **SAVES:** SAVING YOUR POST IMPLIES THAT THERE IS SUCH HIGH VALUE THAT USERS WANT TO SAVE THE POST.

- **IMPRESSIONS:** THE NUMBER OF TIMES YOUR POST IS SEEN, WHICH LETS YOU KNOW HOW MANY PEOPLE IT REACHED.

- **CTR:** IT MEASURES HOW EFFECTIVE THE CALL-TO-ACTION FOR LINKS YOU'RE SHARING IN YOUR THREADS IS.

EXAMPLE: ADIDAS' #HERETOCREATE CAMPAIGN

ADIDAS TOOK INSPIRATION FROM THE #HERETOCREATE CAMPAIGN IN ORDER TO BRING OUT THE INNER ATHLETE.

THEY OBSERVED ENGAGEMENTS IN THE FORM OF LIKES, COMMENTS, AND SHARES TO UNDERSTAND WHICH PART OF THE CAMPAIGN WAS CAUSING MORE ENGAGEMENT WITH THE AUDIENCE.

THEY NOTICED THAT CONTENT INVOLVING A KIND WHERE ATHLETES ARE IN ACTION RESULTS IN HIGH ENGAGEMENT; INSPIRATIONAL QUOTES WORK AS SOMETHING THAT SHARED.

- **STRATEGY:** IDENTIFY THE KIND OF CONTENT THAT GENERATES THE MOST NUMBER OF ENGAGEMENTS (ATHLETE STORIES, PRODUCT SHOWCASES, QUOTAS, ETC.).

- **TAKEAWAY:** MONITORING SUCH METRICS CAN HELP ADIDAS REFINE ITS MESSAGING AND VISUALS OF FUTURE POSTS, FOCUSING ON THOSE THINGS THAT WORKED.

2. A/B TESTING CONTENT VARIATIONS

A/B TESTING IS A PROCEDURE WHERE TWO VERSIONS OF THE SAME POST ARE CREATED. THESE MIGHT DIFFER BY ONE TINY DETAIL: WORDING, IMAGERY, OR FORMATTING, THEN COMPARE HOW EACH PERFORMED. THIS WILL TELL YOU WHICH ELEMENTS PLAY BEST WITH YOUR AUDIENCE.

EXAMPLE: H&M'S FASHION POSTS

H&M TESTED A/B FOR THREADS ON POSTS COMPARING TWO VERSIONS OF THE SAME FASHION PROMOTION, EITHER FEATURING A MODEL OR FLAT-LAY PRODUCT PHOTOGRAPHY.

RESULTS WERE THAT THOSE WITH MODELS MADE THE POSTS MORE ENGAGING, ESPECIALLY IF THE STYLING WAS LESS GLAMOROUS AND MORE LIKE REAL LIFE.

- **TEST:** TRY MULTIPLE VARIABLES SUCH AS POST TYPE (IMAGE OR VIDEO), TEXT LENGTH, AND VISUAL AESTHETICS TO DISCOVER THE PERFECT COMBINATION FOR PERFORMANCE.

- **LEARNING TAKEAWAY:** A/B TESTING ENABLES YOU TO REFINE YOUR POSTS BY FINDING OUT WHAT DOES AND DOESN'T RESONATE WITH YOUR AUDIENCE.

3. MONITOR AUDIENCE FEEDBACK

SCAN THE COMMENTS YOU RECEIVE ON YOUR POST AND CHECK THE SENTIMENT—INCREASED, NEUTRAL, OR DECREASED.

VIEWS FROM AUDIENCES, WHETHER THROUGH A COMMENT OR AN INDIRECT CUE LIKE A SHARE, ENDOW YOU WITH INCREDIBLY VALUABLE INFORMATION ABOUT THE POPULARITY OF YOUR CONTENT.

CASE STUDY: GLOSSIER'S CUSTOMER ENGAGEMENT

GLOSSIER IS A BEAUTY BRAND KNOWN TO PUT EMPHASIS ON USER FEEDBACK AND SUBSEQUENTLY ALIGN FUTURE CONTENT AND PRODUCT LAUNCHES WITH THAT. THEY ARE PAYING ATTENTION TO WHAT CUSTOMERS ARE TALKING ABOUT THEIR PRODUCTS IN COMMENTS, THEN ALTERING THEIR MESSAGING AND PRODUCT POSITIONING.

• PAY CLOSE ATTENTION TO THE COMMENTS AND DMS AND CHECK THEIR SENTIMENT FOR A BETTER UNDERSTANDING OF HOW PEOPLE FEEL ABOUT YOUR CONTENT.

TAKEAWAY: PAY ATTENTION TO AUDIENCE FEEDBACK TO BETTER CALIBRATE MESSAGING AND CONTENT.

4. ANALYTICS TOOLS

TOOLS SUCH AS INSTAGRAM INSIGHTS PROVIDE YOU WITH INFORMATION ABOUT HOW YOUR THREADS ARE DOING, FOR INSTANCE, HOW YOUR POSTS ARE DOING. ANALYTICS TOOLS GIVE YOU AUDIENCE DEMOGRAPHICS, THE RATE AT WHICH THEY ENGAGE, THE REACH, AND MUCH MORE, THUS GIVING YOU ACTIONABLE DATA FOR STRATEGY IMPROVEMENTS.

EXAMPLE: UTILIZING ANALYTICS.

SEPHORA TRACKS HOW CUSTOMERS REACT TO THEIR CONTENT THROUGH INSTAGRAM INSIGHTS AND OTHER ANALYTICS TOOLS, WHERE THEY IDENTIFY CHANGES TO IMPROVE IT.

BASED ON THE INSIGHTS ANALYZED THROUGH INSTAGRAM INSIGHTS, THEY REALIZED THAT MAKEUP TUTORIALS AND PRODUCT RECOMMENDATIONS WERE HIGHLY ENGAGING FOR THE TARGET GROUP.

THREADS' FUTURE CONTENT FOCUSED MORE ON TUTORIALS AND EDUCATIONAL POSTS WITH THIS.

- **STRATEGY:** USE THE ANALYTICS OF YOUR INSTAGRAM TO KNOW WHICH ONE WILL STIMULATE THE MOST ENGAGEMENT, AND THEN CHANGE YOUR STRATEGY ACCORDINGLY.

- **TAKEAWAY:** WITH THE AID OF ANALYTICS TOOLS, YOU CAN MAKE DATA-DRIVEN DECISIONS TO CONSTANTLY UPGRADE YOUR THREADS CONTENT.

6. ENGAGE WITH AUDIENCE ANALYTICS

IDENTIFY WHOM YOUR MOST ENGAGED AUDIENCE MEMBERS ARE. YOU CAN MAKE YOUR THREADS EVEN MORE APPEALING TO THE SPECIFIC DEMOGRAPHICS THAT INTEREST YOU MOST WITH THEIR ENGAGEMENT ON YOUR POSTS.

FOR EXAMPLE, IF YOUR AUDIENCE IS USUALLY MORE ENGAGED BY A PARTICULAR AGE GROUP OR LOCATION, ENSURE THAT YOU PRODUCE FUTURE CONTENT BY TARGETING THEIR INTERESTS.

CASE STUDY: COCA-COLA'S PERSONALIZATION STRATEGY

APPLYING DEMOGRAPHIC DATA TO PERSONALIZE BOTTLES WITH POPULAR NAMES, COCA-COLA'S "SHARE A COKE" CAMPAIGN WAS USED TO CREATE SUCH A BUZZ ON SOCIAL MEDIA THAT EVERYONE WANTED TO HAVE THEIR PICTURE TAKEN WITH THEIR "SHARE A COKE" BOTTLE.

Studying which demographic segments were Threads most engaged in that campaign gave Coca-Cola the ability to refine future campaigns targeted toward younger audiences and to participate more.

- **STRATEGY:** Apply the demographic data from your analytics to customize your Threads· strategy to your most engaged audience segments.

TAKEAWAY: Audience segmentation helps you to create more relevant and significant content about the right crowd.

7. Fine-Tune Timing and Frequency of Posting

Utilizing analytics, discover when your target audience is most active and refine your posting schedule.

An analysis of past Threads can help determine your optimal posting times when engagement is at its peak.

HUBSPOT SOCIAL CONTENT

HUBSPOT TRACKS THE BEST POSTING TIME BASED ON BEHAVIOR IN THEIR AUDIENCE.

THEREFORE, THEY REALIZED THAT POSTS DISTRIBUTED DURING BUSINESS HOURS OF THE WEEKDAYS RECEIVED HIGH ENGAGEMENT FROM THE PROFESSIONAL AUDIENCE.

HUBSPOT ADJUSTED THEIR POSTING SCHEDULE SO THAT POSTINGS SHOULD BE SET DURING PEAK TIMES.

- **TACTIC:** POST AT ACTIVE TIMES FOR YOUR AUDIENCE FOR MORE ENGAGEMENT AND COVERAGE.

. **TAKEAWAY:** POST TO THREADS THE WEEKDAYS AT TIMES WHEN YOUR TARGET AUDIENCE IS THE MOST ACTIVE TO MAXIMIZE VIEWS AND ENGAGEMENT.

8. OPTIMIZE FOR VISUAL WORTH OF AN IMAGE OR VIDEO

DETERMINE HOW WELL YOUR IMAGES AND VIDEOS ARE WORKING IN COMPARISON TO ENGAGEMENT. REALLY THE PICTURES OR VIDEOS BRINGING ENGAGEMENT? TRY SOME OF THE VISUAL FORMATS (IMAGE, INFOGRAPHIC, GIF, ETC.) TO KNOW WHICH ONES WORK BEST

CASE STUDY: APPLE'S PRODUCT LAUNCHES

APPLE IS A SULTAN OF VISUALS. THEY SHARE HIGH-QUALITY IMAGES WITH LOW NOISE WHEN LAUNCHING NEW PRODUCTS, AND THE POSTS ARE ALWAYS GETTING AWESOME ENGAGEMENT. IT FURTHER REFINES ITS STRATEGY BY STUDYING WHICH KIND OF VISUAL CONTENT (FOR EXAMPLE, SLEEK PRODUCT SHOTS OR LIFESTYLE SHOTS) PERFORMS BETTER.

- CONTINUOUSLY MONITOR HOW YOUR VISUAL CONTENT IS PERFORMING AND TEST DIFFERENT KINDS OF VISUALS TO IMPROVE ENGAGEMENT.

TAKEAWAY: ONLY THE BEST, VISUALLY APPEALING POSTS WILL GET ENGAGEMENT, SO YOU MUST ALWAYS CHECK IF YOUR VISUAL DOES ITS WORK.

9. TRY VARIOUS CONTENT FORMATS

IMPROVE YOUR THREADS BY TRYING VARIOUS CONTENT FORMATS, SUCH AS:
- **POLLS**
- **Q&A**
- **BEHIND-THE-SCENES CONTENT**
- **USER-GENERATED CONTENT**
- **TUTORIALS AND HOW-TO'S**

EXAMPLE: GOPRO'S USER-GENERATED CONTENT
GOPRO IS ENCOURAGING USERS TO SHARE CONTENT, AND THE COMPANY FEATURES IT ON THEIR OWN THREADS. THE COMPANY HAS BEEN EXPERIMENTING WITH DIFFERENT TYPES OF USER-GENERATED CONTENT—ACTION SHOTS, TRAVEL FOOTAGE, AND SO ON—TO REFINE WHAT TYPE OF POSTS DRIVE THE MOST ENGAGEMENT.

- **STRATEGY:** TEST DIFFERENT TYPES OF CONTENT AND SEE WHAT WORKS WELL FOR YOUR AUDIENCE, AND THEN HONE YOUR CONTENT MIX ACCORDINGLY.

- **TAKEAWAY:** MIXED CONTENT TYPES KEEP YOUR THREADS EXCITING AND INTERESTING IN THE EYES OF THE AUDIENCE.

CONCLUSION:

ENGAGEMENT METRICS ARE THE ONLY WAY TO TELL AND IMPROVE YOUR INSTAGRAM THREADS. THIS INCLUDES A/B TESTING AND EVEN EXAMINING THE OPINION OF YOUR AUDIENCE AND THE STRATEGY OF THE COMPETITORS.

MAKE USE OF THE ANALYTICS TOOLS OF INSTAGRAM THAT WILL GIVE YOU INSIGHTS ABOUT YOUR PERFORMANCE AS WELL AS THE PREFERENCE OF THE AUDIENCE WITH REGARDS TO TYPE OF CONTENT, ALONGSIDE THE TIME, BEAUTY, AND ATTRACTIVENESS OF THE POSTS.

CONSTANT TESTING OF NEW IDEAS, MAKING DATA-DRIVEN ADJUSTMENTS, AND STAYING RESPONSIVE TO YOUR AUDIENCE ARE SOME OF THE STRATEGIES THAT CAN HELP ENHANCE THE IMPACT OF YOUR THREADS AND CREATE MORE ENGAGING AND VIRALLY VIRAL CONTENT OVER TIME.

OVER ALL SUMMARY: ANALYZE AND REFINE:

- **TRACK ENGAGEMENT:** MONITOR WHICH THREADS PERFORM WELL AND WHY.

- **ADJUST CONTENT:** USE DATA INSIGHTS TO TWEAK YOUR APPROACH FOR FUTURE POSTS.

EXAMPLE OF A SUCCESSFUL "THREADS TO MILLIONS" POST:

A BUSINESS COACH MIGHT POST A THREAD TITLED:

"5 WAYS TO TRIPLE YOUR PRODUCTIVITY IN A WEEK",

FOLLOWED BY A SERIES OF POSTS WITHIN THAT THREAD DETAILING

PRACTICAL TIPS, PERSONAL STORIES, AND ACTIONABLE STEPS, CONCLUDING WITH A CTA LIKE **"COMMENT WITH YOUR FAVORITE TIP OR SHARE HOW YOU'LL START IMPLEMENTING THESE CHANGES TODAY!"**.

THANK YOU

WWW.DOKETS.SHOP

WHY IT WORKS:

- **HIGH ENGAGEMENT:** THREADS ALLOW FOR DEEPER DIVES INTO TOPICS THAT KEEP USERS ENGAGED.

- **PERSONAL CONNECTION:** STORYTELLING AND INTERACTIVE CONTENT CREATE A BOND BETWEEN THE CREATOR AND THEIR AUDIENCE.

- **VIRALITY POTENTIAL:** THE STRUCTURE MAKES IT EASY FOR READERS TO SHARE CONTENT THEY FIND VALUABLE OR ENTERTAINING.

CONCLUSION:

OVERALL, USING A "THREADS TO MILLIONS" STRATEGY ON INSTAGRAM THREADS HELPS CREATORS, INFLUENCERS, AND BUSINESSES SYSTEMATICALLY BUILD A LOYAL AUDIENCE AND INCREASE VISIBILITY, TURNING FOLLOWERS INTO ENGAGED, POTENTIAL CUSTOMERS.

www.ingramcontent.com/pod-product-compliance
Lightning Source LLC
Chambersburg PA
CBHW071147240526
45465CB00024BA/1841